Andy Hampton's

Saxophone
Basics

A method for individual and group learning

For Naomi, Sam and Holly

Accompaniment CD: 0-571-52160-6
contains piano and saxophone accompaniments from the Teacher's book

Saxophone Basics: Teacher's book
Alto saxophone ISBN 0-571-51973-3
Tenor saxophone ISBN 0-571-52973-9

© 2000 by Faber Music Ltd
First published in 2000 by Faber Music Ltd
First amended impression 2001
3 Queen Square London WC1N 3AU
Music processed by Wessex Music Services
Illustrations by Drew Hillier
Design by Nick Flower
Printed in England by Caligraving Ltd

ISBN 0-571-51972-5

To buy Faber Music publications or to find out about the full range of titles available
please contact your local music retailer or Faber Music sales enquiries:

Faber Music Limited, Burnt Mill, Elizabeth Way, Harlow, CM20 2HX England
Tel: +44 (0)1279 82 89 82   Fax: +44 (0)1279 82 89 83
sales@fabermusic.com   fabermusic.com

FABER *ff* MUSIC

CONTENTS

Unless otherwise stated all musical content is by Andy Hampton.

INTRODUCTION

Welcome to *Saxophone Basics.*

And welcome to that most sophisticated of instruments, the saxophone. In less than no time you'll be well on the way to mastering the instrument and able to impress your friends and family with the range of tunes at your finger tips.

To help you on your way, here are a few words of advice:

- There are lots of duets and group pieces in *Saxophone Basics*; as well as practising and performing by yourself, ask other saxophonists to join you, and have fun playing together.

- From day one ask your teacher or somebody else to play the piano parts in the teacher's book; the music will then really come alive.

- Grab every opportunity to perform in public either as a soloist or in a jazz band or orchestra; this is the best way to gain confidence and, after all, one of the main reasons for learning an instrument!

- If you are unsure of anything, always ask your teacher to explain it or, where necessary, re-explain it.

- Look after your instrument. Clean it after use and store it away safely.

- Practise regularly – it's the only way to improve. A little a day should be the rule.

- Go out of your way to listen to and be inspired by experienced sax players. Find out about concerts, broadcasts on the radio and recordings.

And finally … there are lots of helpful suggestions in the course of *Saxophone Basics*, but if you want a tip from me now, don't forget that you are learning to play **music** first and the saxophone second: make sure everything you do on your sax is musical.

I hope you enjoy learning from this book as much as I did writing it.

Andy Hampton

ACKNOWLEDGEMENTS

There are many people who helped me in writing this book. I'd like to thank my young students who acted as guinea pigs for the early drafts. Thank you to my wife, Jenny, and family for putting up with me being in my studio for months and walking around the house humming little tunes all day. I'd also like to thank Catherine Larkin and Anna Rufey for long play-through sessions to help me get a feel of the book as a whole. Most of all I must thank and acknowledge the huge contribution of my editor at Faber Music, Ben Warren. Ben has always been encouraging and accepting of my ideas and I know that the book is all the better for his particular input.

THE SAXOPHONE

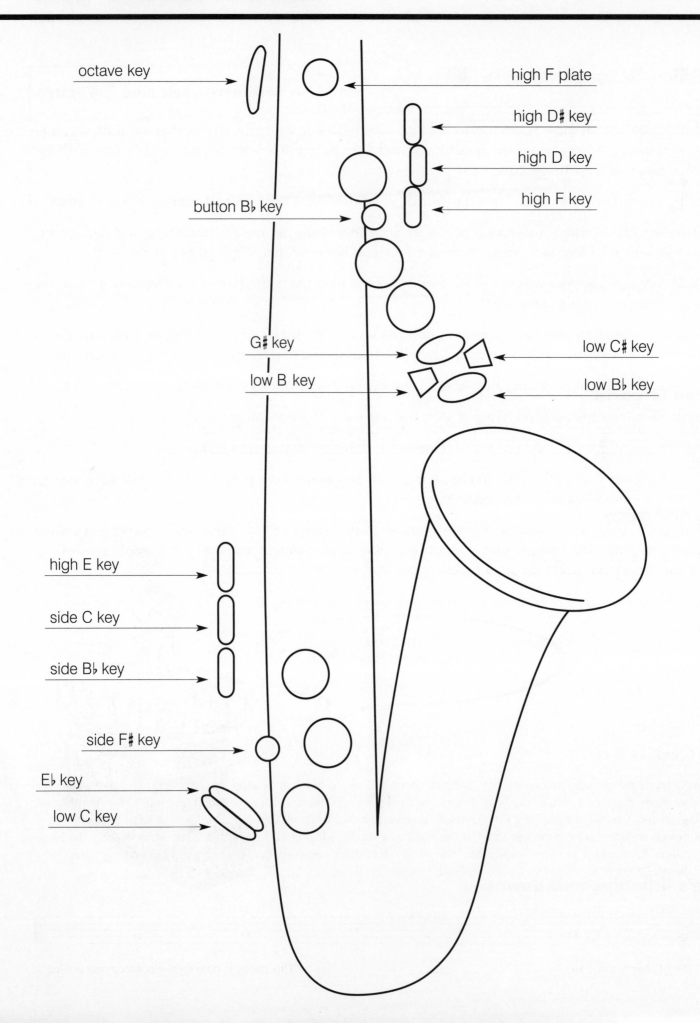

octave key

high F plate

high D# key

high D key

high F key

button Bb key

G# key

low C# key

low B key

low Bb key

high E key

side C key

side Bb key

side F# key

Eb key

low C key

STAGE 1

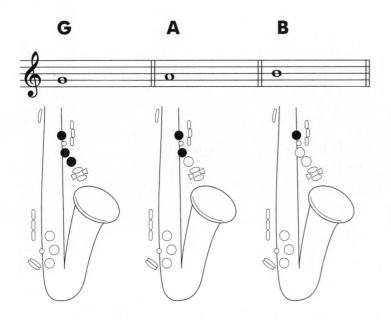

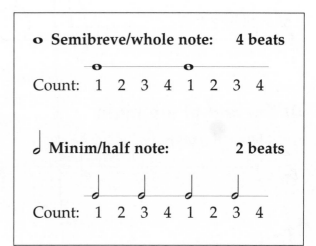

Down to earth

Up and away

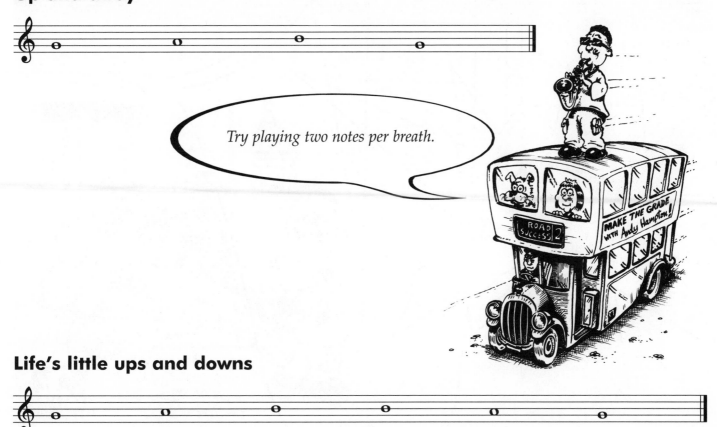

Try playing two notes per breath.

Life's little ups and downs

6

Bitter sweet

At a steady pace

At the end of the night

Slow and stately

Feel the heat

Lively

HOT TIPS
Clean your mouthpiece and reed with a dry cloth before you put your sax away – they can get seriously smelly!

STAGE 2

C

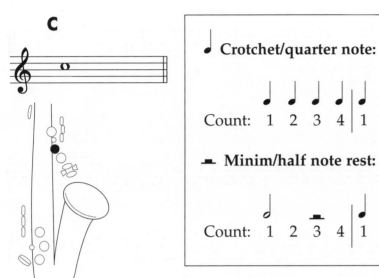

♩ Crotchet/quarter note:	1 beat

Count: 1 2 3 4 | 1 2 3 4

▬ Minim/half note rest:	2 beats

Count: 1 2 3 4 | 1 2 3 4

LONG NOTES

Play each note for a slow count of 4:

How long can you hold each note for?

_____ seconds

count: 1   &   2   &   3   &   4   &

_____ seconds

1   &   2   &   3   &   4   &

_____ seconds

1   &   2   &   3   &   4   &

_____ seconds

1   &   2   &   3   &   4   &

Come join the band

Lively, like a march

And so it goes

Lyrically

Cor blimey

Rhythmically

¿QUIZ?

1 Clap this rhythm:

2 How many beats are there in a 𝅗𝅥 ? _____

3 How long does a ♩ last? _____

4 Why is it a good thing to play long notes?

_____

5 Give your teacher a lesson in how to play tongued notes.

HOT TIPS

*Always put your sax away in its case
when you have finished playing.*

8

STAGE **3**

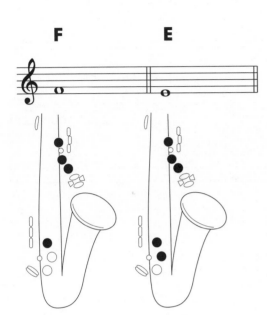

F   **E**

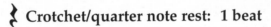

𝄽 Crotchet/quarter note rest: 1 beat

Count: 1 2 3 4 | 1 2 3 4

Theme from the 'New World' Symphony (duet)

Antonín Dvořák

Stately

Part 1

p

Part 2

p

Merrily we blow along

Traditional

Merrily

f

Caribbean Calypso (duet)

Stop FEEF! (duet)

*Not all music starts on the first beat of the bar. Notes that come before the first full bar are called **upbeats**.
Count three beats and come in on beat four.*

Brazilian Girl

HOT TIPS

Check that the height of the strap is correct.

*Practise a little every day rather than one
really long practice every few days.*

STAGE 4

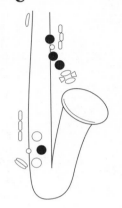

Sorted! (duet)

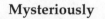

The F♯ Files

Set 'em up

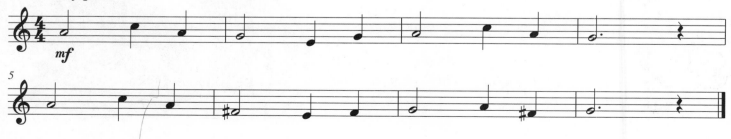

12

This land is my land

Traditional

Medium paced, proud

Cool ghoul

Scarily

¿QUIZ?

1 How long can you blow a Long Note? _____ *seconds*

2 What is a ♩? _____ What is a 𝄽? _____

   What do they have in common? _____

3 What does *f* mean? _____

4 How many beats in this note: ♩. ? _____

5 Explain to your teacher what happens to the
   length of a note when you put a dot after it.

6 Clap this rhythm:

   $\frac{3}{4}$ ♩ ♩ | ♩ ♩ ♩ | ♩ ♩ | ♩. ‖

HOT TIPS
Store your sax away from
direct sunlight and heat.

STAGE 5

D

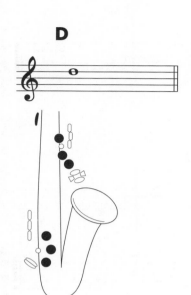

$\frac{2}{4}$ means 2 ♩ beats per bar

Clap: $\frac{2}{4}$ ♩ ♩ ♩ | ♩ | ♩ ♩ | ♩ | ‖

⎯ ▬ ⎯ is a semibreve/ whole note rest.

It lasts for 4 beats, or a whole bar.

As I walked out

At a strolling pace

Sad jazz waltz

Melancholy

14

When the saints

Traditional

Bright and cheerful

Rock that sax!

Hard and loud

About face (duet)

One player plays the music forwards; the other plays it backwards.

First player ⟶

⟵ Second player

Song of the Volga Boatman

Traditional

Slow and strong

HOT TIPS

Three things to remember when practising:

1: At first play the difficult bits slowly so you can be sure to get them right.

2: Do lots of repetition. It's the only way to learn to play the difficult bits.

3: Practise the difficult bits as well as the easier bits.

WRONG NOTES POOR TIME-KEEPING BAD FINGERING DON'T WASTE RECYCLE

STAGE 6

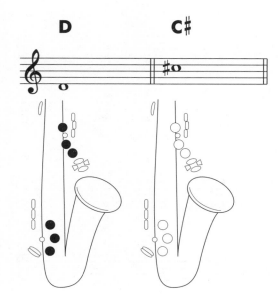

D   C#

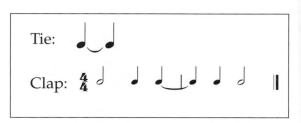

Tie:

Clap:

Razor sharp

Carefully!

HOT TIPS

When you play low notes, try to open your throat and the back of your mouth as much as possible. As you blow imagine you are about to sing a very low note.

That sinking feeling

Medium paced

Deep 'D' duet

Fast

Call of the wild

*The time value of the **upbeats** is taken from the last bar, making it incomplete. Count two beats in.*

At a full gallop

Carnival of Venice

Traditional

Count two beats in.

Lilting

Swanee River

Traditional

Slow and calm

North Pole, South Pole

The 2nd player plays with the book upside down.

Playing by ear …

*See if you can play 'London's Burning',
'Amazing Grace' or 'Happy Birthday' by ear,
without any music.*

Start all three tunes on D.

¿QUIZ?

1   How long is this note: 𝅝 ? _____ beats

2   What does *mf* mean? _____

3   What are you doing when you play *legato*? _____

4   Clap this rhythm:

5   Explain to your teacher the difference between slurred notes and tied notes.

STAGE 7

SCALES

Learning
to play scales
is really important
because they are the
building blocks of music.

Learn them both *legato*
and *staccato* and off by heart.

D major

Try to play this scale in one breath.

Woogie Boogie

Bouncy

mf

A whole lot of soul

Slow and soulful

Dotty mazurka

Very precise

Nobody knows the trouble I've seen

Traditional

Slow and simple

Yankee Doodle (duet)

Traditional

Fairly fast

Part 1

Part 2

HOT TIPS

It's really important to **warm up** before you play: your lips, mouth and throat all need to adjust themselves to the right position for the best sound. The best way to warm up is by playing **long notes** and **scales**.

STAGE 8

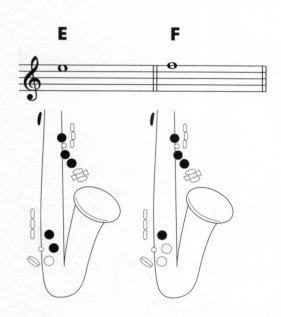

E   F

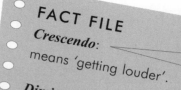

FACT FILE

Crescendo:
means 'getting louder'.

Diminuendo:
means 'getting quieter'.

Andante means 'at a walking pace'.
Moderato means 'at a moderate pace'.
Dolce means 'sweetly'.

Quavers/eighth notes: ¹/₂ beat

Clap: 2/4

> *Arpeggios* are made up of the first,
> the third and the fifth note of the scale.
>
> Make up your own tune using the notes
> of the D major scale. Ask your teacher to
> help you write it down.

D major arpeggio

Lazy days

Moderato

mp

Knock, knock

Fairly quick

It's a cinch

Moderato

Lieutenant Kije

Sergei Prokofiev

Fairly slow

Mo better blues

Bill Lee

Andante

Hatikvah

Jewish traditional

Majestically

Sweet Betsy from Pike

Traditional

Medium paced

Tread on my shadow (duet)

The 2nd player starts one bar after the first.

Brisk pace

Ask your teacher or a pianist to play along with you.

¿QUIZ?

1 What does this sign mean: ⌢ ? _____

2 What does this sign mean: ◁——— ?

_____

3 What are you doing if you are playing *legato*; and *staccato*?

_____   _____

4 Work out how to play *Jingle Bells* by ear, starting on B.

5 Write down the rhythms of the first two 'Jingle bells' in the song.

_____

6 Explain **key signatures** to your teacher.

STAGE 9

B♭ (button)   B♭ (side)

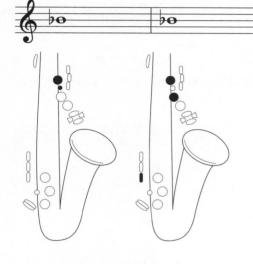

FACT FILE

Swing is a vital ingredient of jazz. When you play swing quavers make the first quaver/eighth note twice as long as the second. To get the feel of swing listen to some jazz songs. *The Pink Panther* is a good starting point.

The **flat sign** ♭ before a note makes it lower by a semitone. A **natural sign** ♮ cancels a sharp or flat. Flats ♭, sharps ♯ and naturals ♮ which occur in a piece and are not part of the key signature are called **accidentals**. Accidentals maintain their effect until the end of the bar.

Allegretto means 'fairly fast'.

♪ **Quaver/eighth note rest:**   ¹/₂ **beat**

Clap:

F major scale and arpeggio

Use the button B♭ fingering.

Which fingering should I use?

Button B♭: *music with no or very few B♮s.*
Side B♭: *music full of B♭ to B♮ steps.*

24

Down the road

Use the button B♭ fingering.

Be happy, be natural, be flat

Use the side B♭ fingering.

Cool 4 cats

Cat's tail swing

Allegretto — swing

HOT TIPS

Work out a musical exercise to help you play 'side B♭' smoothly and easily. Try to make it tuneful and ask your teacher to help you write it down.

STAGE 10

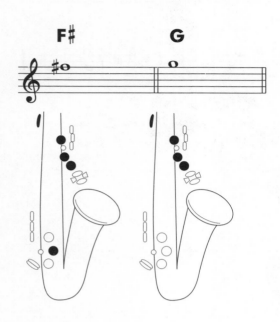

G major scale and arpeggio

The key signature of G major has one sharp (F♯).

G force

Two down, one on the side

The Ashgrove

Traditional

Frankie and Johnny

Traditional

¿QUIZ?

1 What are the notes of an F major arpeggio?

   ____   ____   ____   ____

2 What does an accidental do and how long does it last?

   _____

3 Explain to your teacher when you should use
the 'side B♭' fingering and when the 'button B♭'
fingering.

4 Now play a tune off by heart; choose your own,
or one from this book.

STAGE 11

A

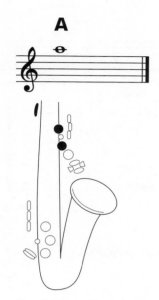

♩. **Dotted crotchet/quarter note: 1¹/₂ beats**

Usually appears as: ♩. ♪

Clap:

D minor scale (harmonic version) and arpeggio

Dee for two (duet)

Moderato

Part 1

mf

Part 2

5

rit.

La follia (duet)

Portuguese Pavane

Green onions

Booker T. Jones, Al Jackson Jnr, Lewis Steinberg, Steve Cropper

Find a friend to play with.

Just left of right

CONCERT PIECES

Vivace

Arcangelo Corelli

Walk the cat

Lay me down

Blue call

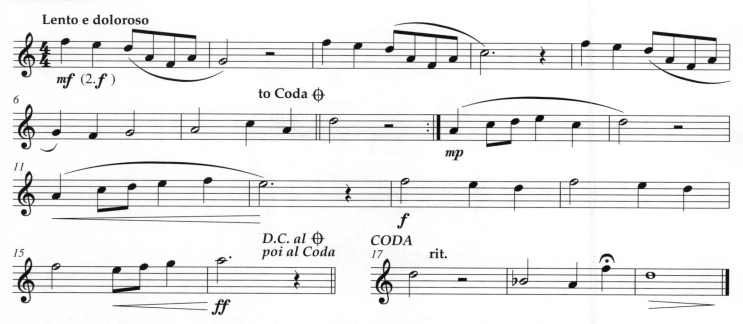

D.C. al ⊕ poi al Coda means go back to the beginning of the piece and play till the sign ⊕ .
When you reach the sign go to the **CODA**.

STAGE **12**

B   **C**   **B♭** (see Stage 9)

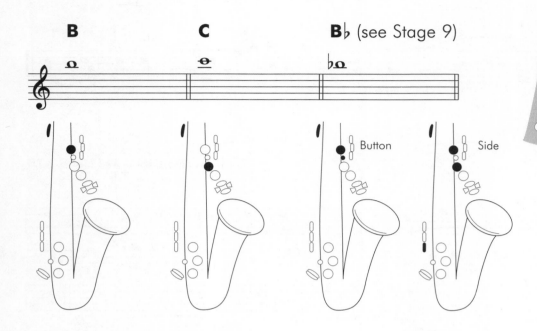

Warm-up bossa (one breath for four bars)

Tempo di bossa nova

Finger twister

Take this slowly at first and then gradually speed up.

Slane

Traditional

Moderato e espressivo

Greensleeves

Traditional, attributed to Henry VIII

Allegretto

One mint julep

Rudolph Toombs

¿QUIZ?

1 How long does a ♩. last for? _____

2 What does *rit.* mean? _____

3 What does *p* mean? _____

4 What is the key signature of G major? _____

5 How many long notes have you played since the last lesson?

_____

Choose one of the ideas from 'Musical games' (page 62) and work at it with your teacher.

STAGE 13

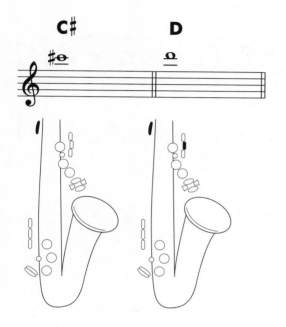

C# **D**

FACT FILE

D.S. al Fine means 'go back to the sign 𝄋 and then play to ***Fine*** where the piece ends'.

Pesante means 'heavy'.

D major scale

D major arpeggio

Start off using the notation but then always learn your scales and arpeggios by heart.

Day and night

Wave them goodbye (duet)

Duetteud

A musical curiosity – this duet works played forwards by one player and backwards by another.

Creepin' around

STAGE **14**

FACT FILE

Triplet quavers/ triplet eighth notes are three, equal-length notes played per ♩ beat.

ff (*fortissimo*) means 'very loud'.

pp (*pianissimo*) means 'very quiet'.

Molto espressivo means 'very expressively'.

C

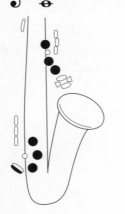

Remember that low notes need plenty of power and a big mouth shape.

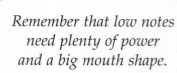

C U down there

Swing (start playing this piece loudly, then gradually more quietly.)

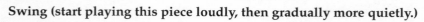

Get out of my way!!!

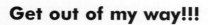

ff

That ship's a long way off yet

pp

Walking past a fog horn

Go with the flow

You and me

¿QUIZ?

1 Explain triplet quavers/eighth notes to your teacher.

2 What is the key signature of D major? _____

3 What is an arpeggio? _____

4 What does **D.S. al Fine** mean? _____

5 How many beats in a ♩. ? _____

6 Choose an idea from 'Composing on the saxophone' (page 64) and write a piece for your next lesson.

STAGE 15

FACT FILE
Because G♯ is both a semitone higher than G and a semitone lower than A, it can also be called A♭. All the sharps and flats can be described in two ways.

G♯   **A♭**

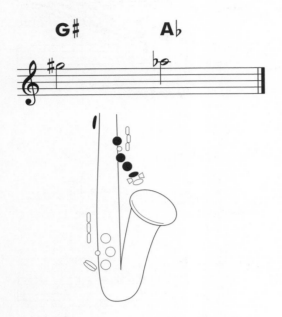

A minor (harmonic version)

A minor arpeggio

Finger twister sister

The King's own dance

Before improvising in these pieces have a look at page 63, 'Improvising on the saxophone'.

Which way now?

44

That swing thing (duet)

DON'T
BE
A SLAVE
TO
NOTATION!

STAGE 16

FACT FILE
Allargando means 'broadening': getting a little slower and perhaps a little louder.

God rest ye merry, gentlemen

Traditional

Merry in May

46

Tell me about it

Here comes the blues

¿QUIZ?

1 What is this note: 🎼 ? _____

2 What is another name for G♭? _____

3 What does this time signature mean: ¢? _____

4 Explain 'swing' to your teacher.

5 Choose another idea from 'Composing on the saxophone' and write a piece for your next lesson.

STAGE **17**

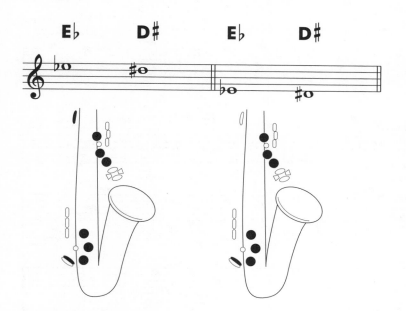

Eb   D#   Eb   D#

> ### FACT FILE
> The **blues scale** will help you play blues.
>
> 1st time and 2nd time bars:
>
> |1.⌐ |2.⌐
>
> The first time through the piece play the '1st time' bars; the second time through, leave out the '1st time' bars and go straight to the '2nd time' bars.
>
> *Morendo* means 'dying away'.

Blues scale in A

Finger twister blister

THROB

I'm late for school!

Wintertime Blues

STAGE 18

C major arpeggio

C major scale

Take your partners, please

A lively dance

After you (duet)

The 2nd player starts one bar after the first.

Allegretto

If I were you (duet)

The shortest blues song ever (duet)

OHHH… I WOKE UP
THIS MORNING…

IT'S MY BIRTHDAY

52

Scarborough Fair

¿QUIZ?

1 Explain $\frac{6}{8}$ time to your teacher.

2 What is another name for A♯? _____

3 What is meant by '1st time' bar and '2nd time' bar?

_____

4 What do the following tempo markings mean?

Allegro _____

Moderato _____

Lento _____

Adagio _____

Choose another idea from
'Musical games' on page 62.

STAGE 19

FACT FILE

Triplet crotchets/ quarter notes.

Play three triplet crotchets/ quarter notes in the time of two normal ♩♩

Theme from 'Red Dwarf'

Howard Goodall

Miami Beach

Richard Harris

54

Allegretto

Gentle and plaintive

Another wet Wednesday

Slow jazz waltz — swing

STAGE **20**

FACT FILE

Notes that go against the beat are called **off beats**. Another name for them is 'syncopated notes'.

Off the beaten track (duet)

Fanfare

Theme from 'Men Behaving Badly'

Alan Lisk

Beethoven's 7th Symphony: 2nd movement

Ludwig van Beethoven

Alone again

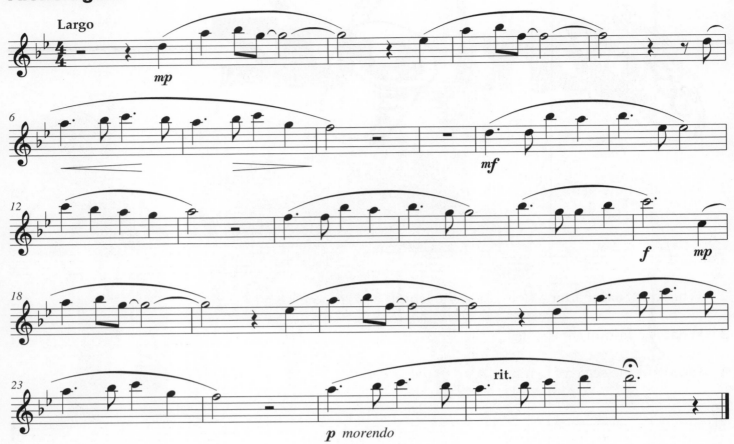

1   Write the note names above the following: (5)

2   What does a dot after a note do to the length of that note? _____ (2)

3   What is a minim/half note? _____ (2)

4   Write out the scale of C major, one octave, ascending.   (8)

5   What does this symbol mean? _____ (2)

6   What does *rit.* mean? _____ (2)

7   Why do we play long notes? _____ (2)

8   What is another name for B♭? _____ (2)

9   How many beats are there in a $\frac{6}{8}$ bar? _____ (2)

10 What are the notes in an F major arpeggio? _____ (3)

11 What is the relative minor of C major? _____ (2)

12 What is syncopation? _____ (2)

13 What is the key signature of D major? _____ (2)

14 What does *allegro* mean? _____ (2)

15 What is the symbol for 'very loud'? _____ (2)

Total   (40)

FINGERING CHART

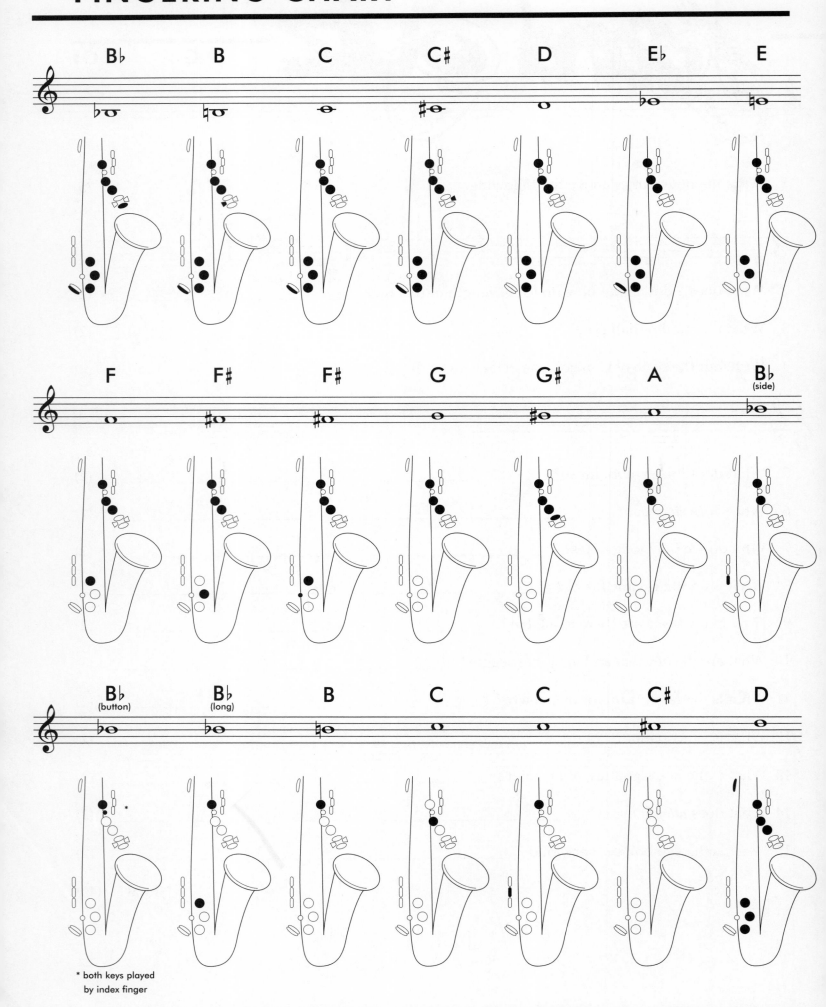

* both keys played
by index finger

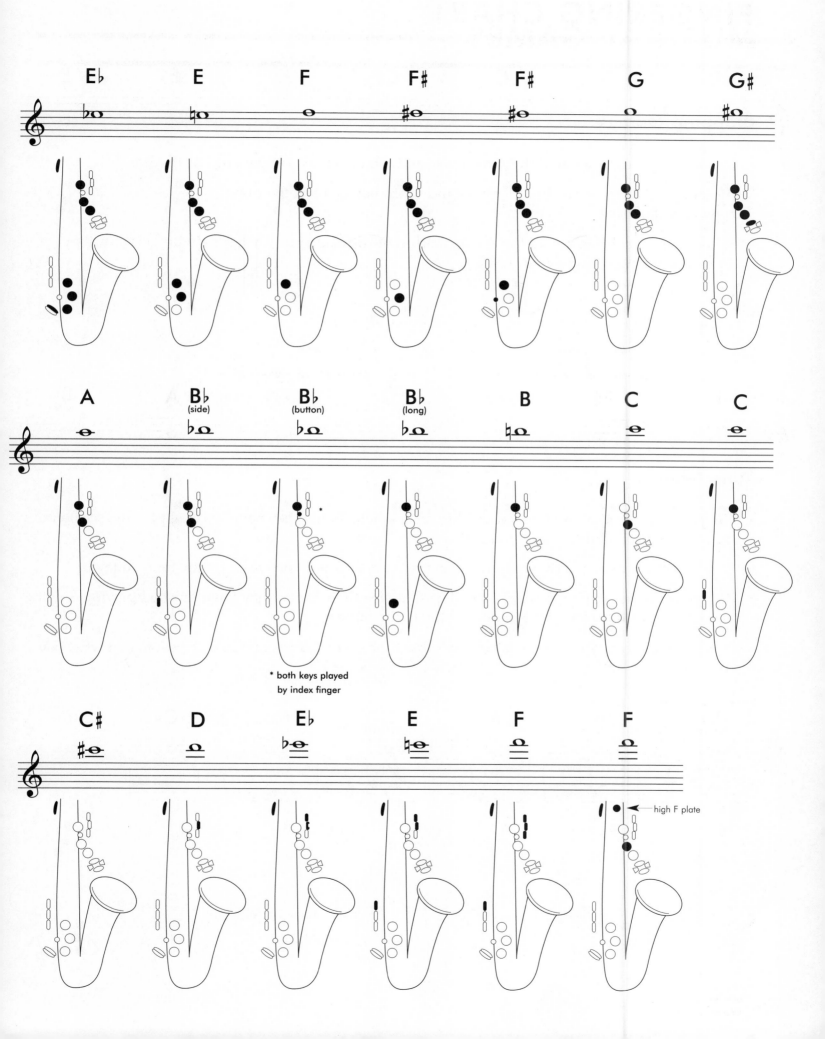

MUSICAL GAMES

Clapping Games

- Get your teacher to set up a rhythmic pulse and then to clap a simple one-bar rhythm.

  As soon as they have finished clapping and when you can feel the pulse,
  copy and clap back the rhythm.

- When you are confident with the above, instead of copying your teacher's rhythm exactly, think of
  a few interesting ways to alter it.

  For example:

Teacher's rhythm   *Your rhythm*

Tune Games

- Get your teacher to play a two-bar rhythm on one note. When they have finished playing, see if you
  can copy and play the rhythm yourself.

- Now ask them to play a two-bar tune using two notes. See if you can copy the tune yourself.

- Ask your teacher to play a simple, two-bar tune this time. When they have finished playing, see if
  you can copy the melody and rhythm of the tune yourself.

- Now instead of copying your teacher's two-bar tune exactly, think of it as a 'question' and what you
  play as an 'answer'.

  For example:

Teacher's question   *Your answer*

IMPROVISING ON THE SAXOPHONE

Before you try this section make sure you have worked at some of the Clapping and Tune games.

When you improvise, instead of playing music off a printed page, you make up your own music as you go along. Improvising is easy and everyone can improvise!

Try these ideas as starting points for your own improvisations:

- First improvise your own four-bar, short piece just using two notes: A and C. Play everything you create rhythmically and without any hesitation or uncertainty; set yourself a pulse, tap it with your foot or move some part of your body in time and then play. Remember – stay in time with the pulse.

- Now try adding B to the A and C; then try A, B, C, D, E and G. Repeat some of your rhythms so that the listener can follow what you are doing.

- Next, take the same notebank – A, C, D, E, G – and ask someone (your teacher, perhaps) to play with you. While you improvise they could play:

Or, on the piano:

- Finally, remember that you get better every time you have a go. Why not do some improvisation as a warm-up at the beginning of a practice or a lesson. Experiment with other sets of notes – scales are good – and ask your teacher to help you find unusual ones.

Here are a few suggestions:

- G, A, B♭, C, D, and F♯

- D, E, F♯, A, and B

- D, C♯, B♭, A, and G

You'll find more opportunities to improvise in Stage 15.

COMPOSING ON THE SAXOPHONE

There is no correct or incorrect way to compose; the only thing that matters is whether the music sounds like you wanted it to sound.

Try these ideas as starting points for your own composing. Ask your teacher to help you by writing your ideas down with you and perhaps finding a piano part to go with your composition.

1   Write a piece inspired by the title
    March of the Zombies.

2   Write a piece using only the notes of
    G major, and which follows the rhythmic
    pattern of *Cat's tail swing* in Stage 9.

3   Write a jazzed-up version of any nursery
    rhyme tune.

4   Write a piece in the key of F major
    which only uses this rhythm:

5   Write a piece in D major beginning and ending on bottom D;
    include top A at some point in the tune.

6   Continue this tune:

7   Write a piece that illustrates the title *Ghost in the junkyard.*
    Experiment with all sorts of special effects available on your instrument,
    for example, blowing noises and squeaks.

8   Write a sad piece. Start on A and only use the notes A, B, C, D, E, and F. Give the piece a title.

9   Write a piece that includes a big moment of surprise. Give the piece a title.

10 Write a piece that is exactly eight bars long and uses the notes A, C, D, E and G.
    Give the piece a title.